THE SISTINE

CHAPEL

ITS HISTORY AND MASTERPIECES

TEXT
VITTORIO GIUDICI

ILLUSTRATIONS
L.R. GALANTE

EDIZIONI MUSEI VATICANI

PETER BEDRICK BOOKS
NTC/Contemporary Publishing Group
NEW YORK

DoGi

Library of Congress Cataloging-in-Publication Data

Giudici, Vittorio.
 The Sistine Chapel : its history and masterpieces / text by Vittorio Giudici ; illustrations by L. R. Galante.
  p.   cm.
 Originally published: Italy : Edizioni Musei Vaticani, 1998.
 Includes index.
 ISBN 0-87226-638-9
 1. Capella Sistina (Vatican Palace, Vatican City)   I. Title.
N2950.G58   2000
726.55'09456'34—dc21   00-29250
                                             CIP

Created by DoGi spa, Florence, Italy

Original title: La cappella Sistina
Concept and Text: Vittorio Giudici
Illustrations: L. R. Galante
Visualization: L.R. Galante and Sergio
Art direction and page design: Sebastiano Ranchetti
Picture research: Katherine Carson Forden
Editing: Andrea Bachini
Translation: Anthony Brierley
© May 1998
Ufficio Vendita Pubblicazioni e Riproduzioni dei Musei Vaticani, 00120 Vatican City

This edition first published in 2000 by Peter Bedrick Books
A division of NTC/Contemporary Publishing Group, Inc.
4255 West Touhy Avenue, Lincolnwood (Chicago), Illinois 60712-1975 U.S.A.
Copyright © 2000 by Ufficio Vendita Pubblicazioni e Riproduzioni dei Musei Vaticani
All rights reserved. No part of this book may be reproduced, stored in a retrieval system, or transmitted in any form or by any means, electronic, mechanical, photocopying, recording, or otherwise, without the prior written permission of the copyright holder.
Printed in Italy
International Standard Book Number: 0-87226-638-9
15 14 13 12 11 10 9 8 7 6 5 4 3 2 1

List of works

Works reproduced in their entirety are indicated with the letter E; those of which only a detail is featured are followed by the letter D.

The works reproduced in this book are listed here, with their date (when known), the place where they are currently housed, and the page number. The numbers in bold type refer to the credits on page 48.

Abbreviations: SC: Sistine Chapel; VM: Vatican Museums.

ANONYMOUS
1. *Laocoon*, 1st century A.D., marble, height 245 cm, copy of the Hellenistic bronze of Agesandros, Atenodorus and Polidorus, 2nd-1st century B.C. (Octagonal Courtyard, VM) 9 E; 2. *Marcellus I*, 1481-82, fresco (Gallery of the Popes, SC) 20 D; 3. *Sixtus I*, 1481-82, fresco (Gallery of the Popes, SC) 21 D; 4. *View of Rome after the interventions of Sixtus V in 1602*, engraving (Raccolta Stampa Archivio Bertarelli, Milan) 8 E

BOTTICELLI (ALESSANDRO FILIPEPI)
5. *Cornelius*, 1481-82, fresco (Gallery of the Popes, SC) 20 D; 6. *Evaristus*, 1481-82, fresco (Gallery of the Popes, SC) 21 D; 7. *Lucius I*, 1481-82, fresco (Gallery of the Popes, SC) 20 D; 8. *Marcellinus*, 1481-82, fresco (Gallery of the Popes, SC) 20 D; 9. *Birth of Venus*, 1484-1486, tempera on canvas, 172 x 278 cm (Uffizi, Florence) 15 D; 10. *Sixtus II*, 1481-82, fresco (Gallery of the Popes, SC) 20 D; 11. *Soter*, 1481-82, fresco (Gallery of the Popes, SC) 21 D; 12. *Stephen I*, 1481-82, fresco (Gallery of the Popes, SC) 20 D; 13. *Stories of Christ: The Temptation of Christ, The Purification of the Leper*, 1481-82, fresco, 335 x 550 cm (SC) 15 E; 14. *Stories of Moses: Punishment of Korah, Dathan and Abiram*, 1481-82, fresco, 335 x 550 cm (SC) 18 E, D; 15. *Stories of Moses: The Burning Bush, Moses Slays the Egyptian; Moses Drives Away the Midianites, Moses Departs for Egypt*, 1481-82, fresco, 335 x 550 cm (SC) 14 E, D

BRAMANTE, DONATO
16. *Tempietto*, c.1502-1510 (San Pietro in Montorio, Rome) 24 E

BROECK, HENDRIK VAN DEN
17. *Resurrection of Christ*, between 1572 and 1585, fresco (SC) 43 E

GHIRLANDAIO (DOMENICO DI TOMMASO BIGORDI)
18. *Anacletus*, fresco, 1481-82, (Gallery of the Popes, SC) 21 E, D; 19. *Angel Appearing to Zacharias*, 1490, fresco, 250 x 450 cm (Tornabuoni Chapel, Santa Maria Novella, Florence) 17 D; 20. *Clement I*, 1481-82, fresco (Gallery of the Popes, SC) 21 D; 21. *Eutychianus*, 1481-82, fresco (Gallery of the Popes, SC) 20 D; 22. *Felix I*, 1481-82, fresco (Gallery of the Popes, SC) 20 D; 23. *Gaius*, 1481-82, fresco (Gallery of the Popes, SC) 20 D; 24. *Hyginus*, 1481-82, fresco (Gallery of the Popes, SC) 21 D; 25. *Pius I*, 1481-82, fresco (Gallery of the Popes, SC) 21 D; 26. *Stories of Christ: Calling of Peter and Andrew*, 1481-82, fresco, 335 x 550 cm (SC) 17 E, D; 27. *Victor I*, 1481-82, fresco (Gallery of the Popes, SC) 21 D; 28. *Zephyrinus*, 1481-82, fresco (Gallery of the Popes, SC) 21 D

MATTEO DA LECCE (MATTEO PÉREZ)
29. *Dispute Over the Body of Moses*, between 1559 and 1565, fresco (SC) 43 E

MELOZZO DA FORLI (MELOZZO DEGLI AMBROGI)
30. *Sixtus IV Nominates Platina*, c.1480, detached fresco transferred onto canvas, 370 x 350 cm (Vatican Pinacoteca, VM) 10 E, D

MICHELANGELO BUONARROTI
31. *Bearded Captive*, 1513-1520, marble, height 263 cm (Galleria dell'Accademia, Florence) 23 E; 32. *Ceiling*, 1508-12, fresco (ceiling, SC) 32-33 E; 33. *Creation of Adam*, 1511-12, fresco (ceiling, SC) 29 D, 31 D, 40 E, 47 D; 34. *Creation of Eve*, 1511-12, fresco (ceiling, SC) 41 E; 35. *Creation of the Sun, Moon, and Plants*, 1511-12, fresco (ceiling, SC) 41 E; 36. *Drunkenness of Noah*, 1508-10, fresco (ceiling, SC) 41 E; 37. *Holy Family with the Young St John (Tondo Doni)*, 1504-1506, tempera on wood, diameter 120 cm (Uffizi, Florence) 23 E; 38. *Lunettes*, 1508-12, frescoes, 3.40 x 6.50 m (SC) 34-35 E; 39. *Moses*, 1515, marble, height 235 cm (San Pietro in Vincoli, Rome) 24 E; 40. *Nude of the Sacrifice of Noah with medallion*, 1508-10, fresco (ceiling, SC) 32 D; 41. *Original Sin and Expulsion from Earthly Paradise*, 1508-10, fresco (ceiling, SC) 41 E; 42. *Pendentives*, 1508-12, frescoes (ceiling, SC) 36, 37 E; 43. *Prophets*, 1508-12, frescoes (ceiling, SC) 39, E; 44. *Separation of Land and Water*, 1511-12, fresco (ceiling, SC) 40 E; 45. *Separation of Light from Darkness*, 1511-12, fresco (ceiling, SC) 40 E; 46. *Sibyls*, 1508-12, frescoes (ceiling, SC) 38, E, D; 47. *Sketches of blocks for the facade of the church of San Lorenzo in Florence*, 1521, ink, 20.4 x 30.3 cm (Casa Buonarroti, Florence) 22 E; 48. *Spandrels*, 1508-12, frescoes (ceiling, SC) 36, 37 E; 49. *The Deluge*, 1508-10, fresco (ceiling, SC) 40 E; 50. *The Last Judgement*, 1536-1541, fresco, 13.70 x 12.20 m (SC) 44 D, 45 E; 51. *The Sacrifice of Noah*, 1508-10, fresco (ceiling, SC) 40 E; 52. *Tomb of Julius II*, 1512-45, marble (San Pietro in Vincoli, Rome) 24 E

PERUGINO (PIETRO DI CRISTOFORO VANNUCCI)
53. *Alexander I*, 1481-82, fresco (Gallery of the Popes, SC) 21 D; 54. *Anicetus*, 1481-82, fresco (Gallery of the Popes, SC) 21 D; 55. *Anteros*, 1481-82, fresco (Gallery of the Popes, SC) 20 D; 56. *Eleutherius*, 1481-82, fresco (Gallery of the Popes, SC) 21 D; 57. *Fabian*, 1481-82, fresco (Gallery of the Popes, SC) 20 D; 58. *Pontianus*, 1481-82, fresco (Gallery of the Popes, SC) 20 D; 59. *Stories of Christ: The Handing Over of the Keys*, 1481-82, fresco, 335 x 550 cm (SC) 18 D, 19 E, D; 60. *Telesphorus*, 1481-82, fresco (Gallery of the Popes, SC) 21 D; 61. *Urban I*, 1481-82, fresco (Gallery of the Popes, SC) 20 D

PERUGINO WITH THE ASSISTANCE OF PINTURICCHIO
62. *Stories of Christ: Baptism of Christ*, 1481-82, fresco, 335 x 550 cm (SC) 15 E, D; 63.

Stories of Moses: Moses with his Wife Zipporah in Egypt, Circumcision of their Son, 1481-82, fresco, 335 x 550 cm (SC) 14 E

RAPHAEL
64. *Portrait of Julius II*, 1512, tempera on wood, 108.5 x 80 cm (Uffizi, Florence) 24 D; 65. *School of Athens*, 1509-10, fresco, base 770 cm (VM) 23 D; 66. *The Miraculous Haul of Fish*, 1515-1517, tapestry, 360 x 400 cm (Vatican Pinacoteca, VM) 42 E, 43 D

ROSSELLI, COSIMO
67. *Callixtus I*, 1481-82, fresco (Gallery of the Popes, SC) 21 D; 68. *Dionysius*, 1481-82, fresco (Gallery of the Popes, SC) 20 D, 21 E; 69. *Stories of Christ: Last Supper*, 1481-82, fresco, 335 x 550 cm (SC) 19 E; 70. *Stories of Moses: Crossing of the Red Sea*, 1481-82, fresco, 335 x 550 cm (SC) 16 E, D

ROSSELLI, COSIMO WITH THE ASSISTANCE OF PIERO DI COSIMO
71. *Stories of Christ: Sermon on the Mount, Healing of the Leper*, 1481-82, fresco, 335 x 550 cm (SC) 17 E; 72. *Stories of Moses: Handing Over of the Tables of the Law, Adoration of the Golden Calf*, 1481-82, fresco, 335 x 550 cm (SC) 16 E

SIGNORELLI, LUCA
73. *Holy Family*, 1490-1500, oil on wood, diameter 124 cm (Uffizi, Florence) 19 E

SIGNORELLI, LUCA WITH THE ASSISTANCE OF BARTOLOMEO DELLA GATTA
74. *Stories of Moses: Moses Gives the Charge to Joshua, Death of Moses*, 1481-82, fresco, 335 x 550 cm (SC) 18 E, D

TITIAN
75. *Pope Paul III with Alessandro and Ottavio Farnese*, 1546, oil on canvas, 210 x 174 cm (Capodimonte Gallery, Naples) 24 D

VERROCCHIO (ANDREA DI MICHELE CIONI)
76. *Head of St Jerome*, c.1460, tempera on paper glued to wood, 49 x 46 cm (Galleria Palatina, Florence) 13 D

Contents

Leading figures

For five hundred years the Sistine chapel has been one of the most important places for the Christian faith and for the entire history of art. The paintings that cover the walls and ceiling of the chapel are unique masterpieces portraying the story of humanity as intended by God, from the Creation to the Last Judgement. Many prominent figures have contributed to the construction, decoration and history of the chapel. Two popes of the Della Rovere family, Sixtus IV and Julius II, more than anyone else, were responsible for making the chapel into the building we know today. The artists who gave expression to their projects were some of the greatest names in 15th-century painting—Perugino, Botticelli, Signorelli and Ghirlandaio—but the real giant among them was Michelangelo Buonarroti, the creator of the ceiling frescoes and the Last Judgement. In recent years master craftsmen have contributed to restoring these frescoes to their original splendor.

The conclave
In the 20th century the Sistine chapel has been the place used for the election of the pope by the college of cardinals.

Perugino, Botticelli and Pinturicchio
Pietro Perugino and Sandro Botticelli, two of the greatest Italian artists of the 15th century, worked with Pinturicchio on some of the frescoes representing scenes from the Stories of Moses and Christ, paintings that were commissioned by Sixtus IV.

Cosimo Rosselli and Piero di Cosimo
Receiving their artistic training in a workshop that was different from that of Perugino and Botticelli, but of no less solid Florentine tradition, these two artists also took part in the painting of the frescoed stories of Moses and Christ.

Matteo da Lecce and Van den Broek
In the second half of the 16th century these artists were called to repaint two frescoes that had been destroyed.

The restorers
In the second half of the 20th century, and particularly in the 1980s, an extensive cleaning program was undertaken on the painted decoration of the chapel.

A lansquenet
In 1527 Rome was sacked by the troops of the Emperor Charles V, an event in which the Sistine chapel was also involved.

Ghirlandaio and Granacci
Domenico Ghirlandaio was another of the great Florentine masters of the 15th century who took part in the early decoration of the Sistine chapel. Francesco Granacci was a friend of Michelangelo; he introduced him into Ghirlandaio's workshop and was his assistant in the Sistine decoration.

Julius II, Sixtus IV and Michelangelo
Pope Sixtus IV ordered the building of the chapel named after him. His nephew Julius II commissioned Michelangelo to paint the frescoes of the ceiling.

Bartolomeo della Gatta, Signorelli and Raphael
Two generations of Umbrian artists participated in the decoration of the Sistine chapel. Raphael executed the cartoons for the tapestries, which are occasionally hung on the walls.

Vatican Museums
The Papal Museums and Galleries were formed over four centuries and comprise various collections of antiquities—the largest of their kind in the world: the Tapestry Gallery, the Gallery of Maps, Raphael's Stanze, the collection of Modern Religious Art and the ethnological collections.

Sistine Chapel
Situated in the very heart of the Vatican between the Basilica, the Apostolic Palace and the museum complex.

Belvedere Courtyard
According to Bramante's original design (ca. 1505) it occupied the entire area between the Apostolic Palaces and the summer residence (Belvedere) which Innocent VIII (1484–1492) had built to the north of the Vatican hill. The inner garden of Innocent's Palazzetto, which Bramante transformed into a square courtyard, was the world's first open-air museum of classical sculptures.

Walls of the Vatican City
Built for the first time by Leo IV in the 9th century, the present walls are those that Nicholas V had built in the middle of the 15th century.

St. Peter's Basilica
The original basilica was built by the Emperor Constantine in the 4th century over St. Peter's tomb. Michelangelo's project of returning to Bramante's idea of a central-plan temple, conceived as a base for supporting the great cupola, was later modified under Paul V (1605–1621) into the Latin cross we see today.

St. Peter's Square
This vast elliptical space is encircled by four rows of columns linked to the basilica by two porticoes. It was designed in the 17th century by Bernini to allow a greater number of worshippers to see the Pope during the blessing.

Places

The Sistine chapel is situated in the very heart of the Vatican City State, near St. Peter's Basilica. Its ground-plan is extremely simple: a rectangular hall measuring 131 feet in length and 43.5 feet in width, the same proportions the Bible attributes to Solomon's temple in Jerusalem. The building that contains the chapel is divided into four stories: a basement; a mezzanine with nine barrel-vaulted rooms; the chapel itself, 67 feet at the highest point of the famous barrel vault; and a large attic at the top. The height of the edifice, the high position of the windows and particularly the galleries along the sides of the attic give the building the appearance of a small fortress.

Outer view of the Sistine Chapel
This gives a clearer idea of the building's characteristic appearance as a small fortified construction: an outpost of the Vatican Palaces.

Michelangelo's ceiling
Above the third cornice, around the windows and over the entire ceiling are the figures frescoed by Michelangelo.

The gallery of popes
The larger middle cornice forms a gallery along three sides of the chapel: between the 12 windows are 28 portraits of popes.

The 15th-century frescoes
Between the first and second cornice of the side walls are the 12 frescoes painted in the 15th century.

False drapery
According to 15th-century custom, the lowest part of the decoration consists of trompe l'oeil curtains.

The chapel
The pavement is made of polychrome marble. A screen separates the two areas reserved for the congregation and the clergy.

The mezzanine
Divided into nine rooms occupied by the offices of the Masters of Ceremonies.

The basement
This was divided up into nine rooms.

The guards
The large attic above the ceiling of the chapel gave access to the side galleries used by the chapel guards.

The Last Judgement
On the end wall behind the altar is Michelangelo's large fresco representing the Last Judgement.

Rome in the 15th century

Ruler of the ancient world and for centuries capital of a vast empire, with the advent of Christianity the city became the seat of the supreme religious authority, the pope. From the time of the first Christian emperor Constantine, in the 4th century, Christian buildings began to appear among Rome's imperial architecture and pagan monuments. On the site of St. Peter's tomb, Constantine had the basilica dedicated to the Apostle built. In the following centuries, despite the fall of Rome and the desertion of the city, the basilica was even enlarged. In the 15th century, during the papacies of Martin V and Nicholas V, the city experienced a great revival and at the same time its ancient ruins were visited and studied by artists and scholars. This new interest in the past heralded one of the most remarkable periods in human culture: the Renaissance.

Rescuing works of art
During excavations at the foot of the Capitol in Rome, a Corinthian capital is being cleaned. It is all that remains of a temple of Concord from the 4th century BC. It will serve as a model for drawings, measurements and proportions.

Rome
In the 15th and 16th century, after a long period of decline, the city's population and cultural prestige increased.

Study and imitation
Rome, with its immense heritage of ancient ruins, was a great attraction for artists from the early 15th century. Brunelleschi and Donatello went there from Florence in 1402.

The ruins
The remains of some Ionic columns that may once have belonged to a temple dedicated to Saturn.

Laocoon
Excavated and carefully analysed, the statues of antiquity attracted the attention of a great many artists. In 1506, a marble statue of the 1st century AD, 8 feet high, was found near the basilica of Santa Maria Maggiore in Rome. It was the copy of a famous bronze of the Hellenistic period representing Apollo's priest and his sons being killed by two serpents. Vatican Museums, Rome

The changes made by Christianity
Columns of the temple of Antoninus and Faustina, which in the 11th century was converted into a Christian church, San Lorenzo in Miranda.

Melozzo da Forlì, *Sixtus IV*, ca. 1480; detached fresco transferred onto canvas, 370 x 350 cm (12 ft., 2 in. x 11 ft., 6 in.), Vatican Pinacoteca, Rome, detail.

Life of Sixtus IV
Francesco della Rovere (Celle Ligure 1414–Rome 1484) was born into a noble family and belonged to the Franciscan order of friars of whom he was elected general in 1464.
Elected pope in 1471, Sixtus IV was a true Renaissance prince. In the exercise of temporal power he was autocratic and ambitious, and showed a tendency to favor members of his own family. He attempted to rally the European states against the Ottoman Empire. He patronized culture and the arts. He transferred the Vatican library to new premises, enriched it with Greek, Latin and Hebrew works and appointed as its librarian the humanist scholar Bartolomeo Secchi, called Platina. In the sphere of religion he reformed the mendicant orders and conferred greater solemnity to the celebration of the Immaculate Conception.

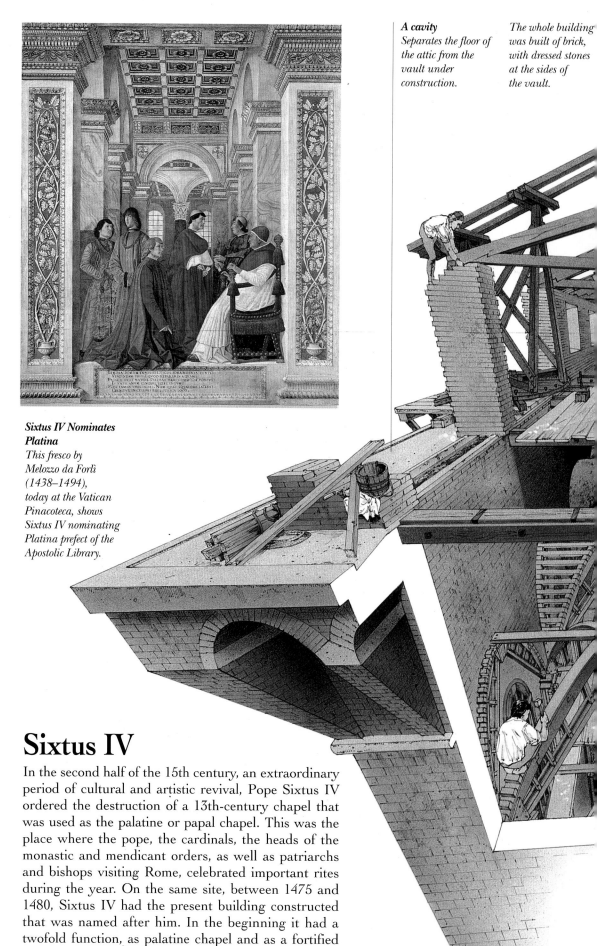

Sixtus IV Nominates Platina
This fresco by Melozzo da Forlì (1438–1494), today at the Vatican Pinacoteca, shows Sixtus IV nominating Platina prefect of the Apostolic Library.

A cavity
Separates the floor of the attic from the vault under construction.

The whole building was built of brick, with dressed stones at the sides of the vault.

Sixtus IV

In the second half of the 15th century, an extraordinary period of cultural and artistic revival, Pope Sixtus IV ordered the destruction of a 13th-century chapel that was used as the palatine or papal chapel. This was the place where the pope, the cardinals, the heads of the monastic and mendicant orders, as well as patriarchs and bishops visiting Rome, celebrated important rites during the year. On the same site, between 1475 and 1480, Sixtus IV had the present building constructed that was named after him. In the beginning it had a twofold function, as palatine chapel and as a fortified outpost of the oldest nucleus of the Vatican palaces.

The attic
Reserved for the guards, the attic leads into the side galleries, which are supported by long corbels. Above the corbels the battlements have arrow-slits and loopholes for defense.

The vault
One of the first made from a concrete mixture of sand, lime and stone aggregate.

A visit
Pope Sixtus IV visits the building site with the Florentine architect Giovannino de' Dolci, who designed the chapel.

The Florentine workshop

When work on the building of the chapel had finally been completed, Sixtus IV turned his attention to the question of its interior decoration. The ornamentation of the great ceiling originally consisted of a simple starry sky, a work attributed to Pier Matteo D'Amelia. For the walls, a more ambitious program was conceived and for this the pope looked to the artists of the Florentine school. The importance of the chapel and the short time the aging pope thought he still had to live prompted him to summon to Rome the most famous workshops and their masters. Most of the artists had trained under Verrocchio. Let us imagine entering his workshop around 1470. Here, we would have found Leonardo da Vinci, Botticelli, Perugino and Ghirlandaio, together with illustrious collectors busy admiring the most varied work: paintings, sculpture, goldworking, and much experimentation with new machines.

Filippo Brunelleschi, Cupola of Santa Maria del Fiore, 1418–1436; Florence.

Florence
In the second half of the 15th century Florence was one of the great centers of European culture. About a century before, the plague that had swept through the continent had halved the city's population, but Florence had reacted and had continued to thrive as one of the world's leading commercial centers.
In the 15th century the city enjoyed a long period of political stability, which corresponded to many years of flourishing artistic activity. Florence was the cradle of Humanism and the Renaissance: here Brunelleschi and Masaccio produced their masterpieces; here, great banking and merchant families, first among them the Medici, commissioned churches, palaces and hospitals to be built, and enriched the city with works of art. The crowning glory of the city's cathedral was a dome of majestic size and beauty.

Leonardo da Vinci
Entered Verrocchio's workshop in 1469 at the age of seventeen. Here he was fascinated by the working of winches and gear mechanisms.

The client
A rich Florentine merchant, art patron and art collector, visits the workshop of Verrocchio. Wealthy Florentines of the 15th century often started by donating objects to churches of the city, then later they became art collectors.

Perugino
Recently arrived from his native Umbria, Perugino experimented with sculpture in terracotta.

Botticelli
Age twenty-four, after two years of apprenticeship with Verrocchio, he opened his own workshop.

The furnace
Inside the workshop was a fully-equipped bronze foundry: an iron-domed stone smelting furnace with air vents and a pouring spout.

Andrea del Verrocchio, *Head of St. Jerome*, ca. 1460; tempera on paper glued to wood, 49 x 46 cm (19.3 x 18 in.), Galleria Palatina, Florence.

Verrocchio
The Florentine painting tradition enjoyed a prestige and level of achievement that was unrivalled, from Giotto, the founder of Italian painting between the 13th and 14th centuries, to Masaccio and the great masters of the 15th century. However, we should not forget the important role of lesser-known masters, those in whose workshops the great masters learned the basic principles of the Florentine school. Among them was Andrea di Cione, called Verrocchio (Florence 1435– Venice 1488), the master of Leonardo da Vinci and many of those artists whom Sixtus IV summoned to fresco the Sistine chapel. Goldsmith, sculptor, painter, draftsman, engineer, and expert in the procedures of bronze casting, for the Venetian Republic Verrocchio executed the great equestrian statue of Bartolomeo Colleoni.

Ghirlandaio
With the precocity typical of Renaissance artists, the thirty-year-old Domenico Ghirlandaio engages in conversation with the older masters.

The masters
Verrocchio receives a visit from Antonio Benci, also known as Pollaiolo (seated on his left). Both men are under forty, but are masters of the two most famous workshops in Florence.

The lavabo
Two workers assemble the marble pieces for the lavabo of the Old Sacristy in San Lorenzo.

Life of Moses

Sixtus IV had the Sistine chapel built to the same size as the temple of Jerusalem, which was built by Solomon and burned down by the Romans in 70 AD. The iconographical program conceived by Sixtus IV was intended to be a comparison between the Old and New Testaments, between the lives of Moses and Christ, and even between Solomon and Sixtus himself. It aimed to represent the continuity, but also to underline the evolution, of the Christian religion over Mosaic law. On the left wall of the chapel, looking towards the altar, from right to left, are scenes from the life of Moses. This is how it now is for modern visitors; originally, however, both cycles began with frescoes on the end wall, which were later destroyed to make space for the Last Judgement.

Botticelli,
Stories of Moses,
detail.

The two stories
The twelve 15th-century frescoes facing each other on the side walls, each measuring 335 x 550 cm (11 x 18 ft.), are grouped into two matching cycles. The stories proceed chronologically, except at the beginning. The first scene from the life of Moses, showing the episode of his son's circumcision (fig. 1), refers to events that came after those of the second scene.
The decoration is intended to draw a comparison: the first is between the *Circumcision of Moses' Son* (fig. 1) and the *Baptism of Christ* (figs. 3 and 3.1). In the second of the two frescoes are other scenes: John speaking of the Messiah to the crowd, John descending into Jordan, and Jesus speaking of the Baptist. The *Temptation of Christ* (fig. 4)—with Satan conversing with Jesus, taking him to the roof of the temple and lastly leading him to the top of a mountain— contrast with those of Moses (figs. 2, 2.2), in which the prophet slays the Egyptian (fig. 2.2), marries one of Jethro's daughters, and lastly sets out for Egypt to free his people (fig. 2.1).

1

2

2.1

2.2

Perugino and Pinturicchio
1. Stories of Moses:
Moses with his Wife Zipporah in Egypt, Circumcision of their Son.

Botticelli
2. Stories of Moses:
The Burning Bush, Moses Slays the Egyptian, Moses Drives Away the Midianites, Moses Departs for Egypt.
In figures 2.1 and 2.2, two details.

Botticelli,
Birth of Venus,
1484–1486; tempera
on canvas, 172 x
278 cm (5 ft., 8 in. x
9 ft., 1 in.), Uffizi,
Florence, detail.

The masters
Pietro Vannucci,
known as Perugino
(Castel della Pieve,
Perugia ca. 1450–
Fontignano,
Perugia 1523). He
frequented the
workshop of
Verrocchio in
Florence and
worked in the
Sistine chapel from
1481 to 1482. His
works include the
Pietà (Uffizi,
Florence), the
Enthroned Madonna
(Louvre, Paris),
and the *Adoration of
the Magi* (Galleria
Nazionale dell'
Umbria, Perugia).

Alessandro Filipepi,
known as Botticelli
(Florence
1445–1510).
In his home town
he had close links
with the Medici.
His works include
the *Primavera* and
the *Birth of Venus*.
A pupil of Filippo
Lippi, and later of
Verrocchio, his art
is distinguished
by the prime
importance given
to the use of
drawn outlines.

Bernardino
di Betto, known as
Pinturicchio
(Perugia ca. 1454–
Siena 1513).
He worked with
Perugino and was
very successful
in Rome.

Life of Christ

On the right wall of the chapel, from left to right, is the story of the life of Christ. Each scene of the narrative is matched by an episode from the life of Moses on the opposite wall. The inscriptions appearing on them invite the congregation to dwell on the meanings of each pair of frescoes. For example, the first scenes of the two stories compare the rite of circumcision in the Old Testament with the rite of Baptism in the New. The triumph of the New over the Old is recalled to the congregation every time differences are illustrated between the lives of Moses and Christ: that which in the Old Testament is represented as bloody, like the sacrifice of the animal, in the New Testament is conveyed as something spiritual and symbolic, like the Baptism and the Eucharist.

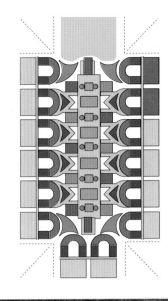

*Perugino
and Pinturicchio*
3. Stories of Christ:
Baptism
of Christ.
*In figure 3.1,
a detail.*

Botticelli
4. Stories of Christ:
The Temptation
of Christ, The
Purification
of the Leper.

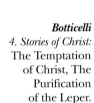

5

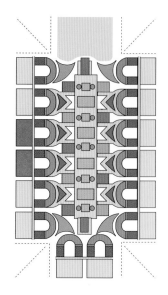

Cosimo Rosselli, *Stories of Moses*, detail.

The two stories
The calling of Peter and Andrew, who abandon their fishing-nets to follow Christ, and of James and John (fig. 7.1) are scenes from the *Stories of Christ* representing the calling of the first apostles (fig. 7).
The scenes face the *Crossing of the Red Sea* on the opposite wall (fig. 5.1): on the far right the pharaoh holds council; then the Egyptian army is engulfed by the sea (fig. 5) and the Israelites are saved. The events of the Old Testament therefore prefigure the later Christian events. Thus, the *Handing Over of the Tables of the Law* (fig. 6) corresponds to the *Sermon on the Mount* (fig. 8).
The harshness of the images in the first of the two frescoes — Moses's violent reaction to the idolatry of his people — corresponds in the second fresco to the image of Christ's love as he heals the leper.

5.1

Cosimo Rosselli
5.1 Stories of Moses:
Crossing of the Red Sea.
In figure 5, a detail.

6

Cosimo Rosselli and Piero di Cosimo
6. Stories of Moses:
Handing Over of the Tables of the Law, Adoration of the Golden Calf.

7

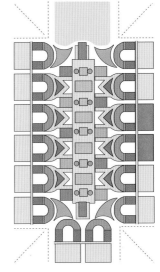

**Domenico
Ghirlandaio**
*Angel Appearing to
Zacharias*, 1490;
fresco, 250 x 450 cm
(8 ft., 2 in. x 14 ft.,
9 in.), Santa Maria
Novella, Florence,
detail.

The masters
Cosimo Rosselli
(Florence
1439–1507).
He set up his own
workshop at an
early age and
painted numerous
altarpieces, like the
Sacra Conversazione
(Uffizi, Florence).
He combined
an interest in
perspective with
a great eye
for detail.

Domenico Bigordi,
known as
Ghirlandaio
(Florence
1449–1494).
He trained in the
workshop of
Verrocchio,
and was very
popular in the later
years of his life.
He is famous for
having been the
painter who most
accurately
portrayed the
habits and customs
of his time, and for
having been for a
short period the
master of
Michelangelo.

Piero di Lorenzo,
known as Piero di
Cosimo (Florence
1461–1521).
A pupil of Cosimo
Rosselli, from
whom his own
name is derived.

7.1

7.2

***Domenico
Ghirlandaio***
7. *Stories of Christ:*
Calling of Peter
and Andrew.
*In figures 7.1
and 7.2, details.*

***Cosimo Rosselli
and Piero di
Cosimo***
8. *Stories of Christ:*
Sermon on the
Mount, Healing
of the Leper.

8

Perugino,
Stories of Christ,
detail.

The two stories
The comparison
between the
Old and New
Testaments
continues in the
last frescoes of the
two side walls.
On one side, in the
*Punishment of
Korah, Dathan, and
Abiram* (fig. 9.1),
the rebels are
shown being
swallowed up by
the earth (fig. 9).
This is matched, in
the *Handing Over of
the Keys* (figs. 11
and 11.1), by the
idea of forgiveness
and salvation in
the Church of
Christ. The last
two scenes
represent the
Testament of Moses
(10 and 10.1) and
the *Last Supper*
(fig. 12). While
Moses hands over
the staff of
leadership to
Joshua (fig. 10.1),
Christ, in the Last
Supper, hands
down himself. The
last two scenes on
the entrance wall
of the chapel
represented the
*Resurrection of
Christ* by
Ghirlandaio, and
the *Dispute over the
Body of Moses* by
Signorelli. Both
paintings were
destroyed when
the entrance wall
collapsed in 1522
and were replaced
in the late 16th
century by works
that are described
on pages 42 and
43 of this book.

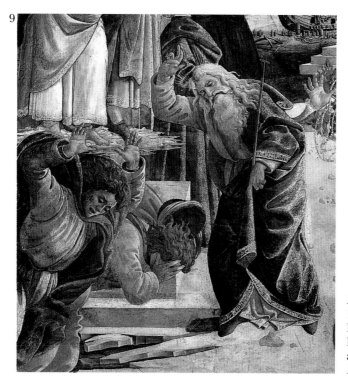

9

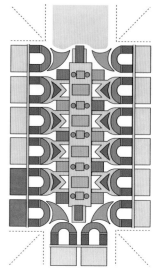

Botticelli
9.1 Stories of Moses:
Punishment of
Korah, Dathan
and Abiram.
In figure 9, a detail.

9.1

10

10.1

**Luca Signorelli
with the assistance
of Bartolomeo
della Gatta**
10. Stories of Moses:
Moses Gives the
Charge to Joshua,
Death of Moses.
*In figure 10.1,
a detail.*

Luca Signorelli, *Holy Family*, 1490–1500, oil on wood, diameter 124 cm (4 ft.), Uffizi, Florence.

The masters
Luca Signorelli (Cortona, Arezzo ca. 1445–1523). A pupil of Pietro Perugino, he also drew inspiration from the teaching of Verrocchio. After a period spent in Florence at the court of Lorenzo de' Medici, and impressed by the preaching of the Dominican friar Girolamo Savonarola, Signorelli painted his masterpiece—the *Last Judgement*— an apocalyptic fresco cycle in six large lunettes that decorate the side wall of Orvieto cathedral.

Pietro Dei, known as Bartolomeo della Gatta (Florence 1448–1502). A friar of the Camaldolensian order, he also came from Verrocchio's circle. In the Sistine chapel he worked both with Perugino and with Signorelli. A painter of great talent, he seemed to draw on many of the different styles and tendencies of his time.

11

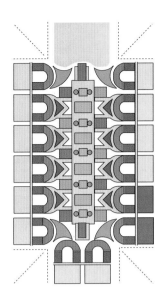

11.1

12

Perugino
11.1 *Stories of Christ:* The Handing Over of the Keys. *In figure 11, a detail.*

Cosimo Rosselli
12. *Stories of Christ:* Last Supper.

Dionysius
(260–268)
Rosselli

Stephen I
(254–257)
Botticelli

Cornelius
(251–253)
Botticelli

Anteros
(235–236)
Perugino

Urban I
(220–230)
Perugino

Eutychianus
(275–283)
Ghirlandaio

Marcellus I
(306–308)
Unattributable

Marcellinus
(296–304)
Botticelli

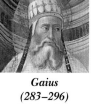

Gaius
(283–296)
Ghirlandaio

1

2

The popes
Popes Marcellus I, Gaius, Marcellinus, and Eutychianus are on the entrance wall of the chapel. The other 24 are

arranged on the side walls, in chronological order, alternating from right to left, from the point nearest the wall behind the altar.

Gallery of the Popes

In the upper fasciae of three walls of the Sistine chapel, above the frescoes depicting the stories of Moses and Christ, are 14 windows. At the sides of the windows are 28 false niches, about 250 cm high, each containing the portrait of a pope. The figures are painted in vivid colors and in a range of lively poses. The completion of the decoration wanted by Sixtus IV is therefore a celebration of his earliest predecessors. The result is a perfect accord between the use of the chapel for papal rites and, much later, for the election of popes, and the presence of a gallery dedicated to them.

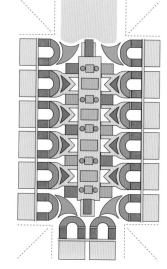

Felix I
(269–274)
Ghirlandaio

Sixtus II
(257–258)
Botticelli

Lucius I
(253–254)
Botticelli

Fabian
(236–250)
Perugino

Pontianus
(230–235)
Perugino

Zephyrinus
(199–217)
Ghirlandaio

Eleutherius
(175–189)
Perugino

Anicetus
(155–166)
Perugino

Hyginus
(136–140)
Ghirlandaio

Sixtus I
(115–125)
Unattributable

3

The gallery of popes
Executed by the same workshops that were painting the fresco cycle below. Only two of the portraits, which were repainted at a later date, are by unknown artists. The sequence of popes originally began from the altar wall, today occupied by the Last Judgement. Here there were representations of Christ, Peter, Linus and Anacletus. There is an obvious link between the gallery of popes, particularly the martyred ones, and the fresco cycle beneath. The stories of Moses and Christ highlight the theme of priesthood and the struggle against heresy, the natural conclusion of which is the glorification of the popes. Figs. 1 and 2: Perugino, Urban I, *details. Figs. 3 and 4: Cosimo Rosselli,* Dionysius; *Domenico Ghirlandaio,* Anacletus.

4

6

Evaristus
(97–105)
Botticelli

Clement I
(88–97)
Ghirlandaio

Anacletus
(76–88)
Ghirlandaio

Alexander I
(105–115)
Perugino

Callixtus I
(217–222)
Rosselli

Victor I
(189–199)
Ghirlandaio

Soter
(166–175)
Botticelli

Pius I
(140–155)
Ghirlandaio

Telesphorus
(125–136)
Perugino

Michelangelo

Michelangelo Buonarroti, sculptor, painter, architect—in short, one of the greatest geniuses of the Renaissance—was born in Tuscany in 1475, the same year in which it is believed Sixtus IV started the building of the Sistine chapel. Raised in the Florence of Lorenzo de' Medici, he devoted much of his time to the study of figures in classical art, and nurtured a profound love of sculpture. For his own works he personally chose marble blocks from the quarries of Carrara. Michelangelo spent much of his long life in solitude—partly in Florence, where he worked in San Lorenzo and defended the Republic as a military architect, and partly in Rome where, patronized by several popes, he left his greatest masterpieces, including the new basilica of St. Peter's and its dome.

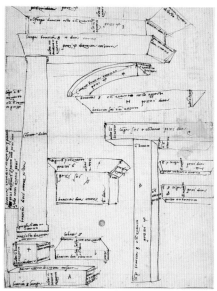

Instructions for the quarrymen
Michelangelo supplied the marble quarrymen with drawings of the blocks, indicating the dimensions and the number of pieces to be prepared.
This sketch, dating from 1521 and conserved in the Casa Buonarroti in Florence, relates to supplies for the facade of the Florentine church of San Lorenzo.

Marble
Marble had been used for sculpture ever since classical times. It was preferred to ordinary stone because it gave a smooth and shiny finish that was well-suited to statues.

In the Apuan Alps
To choose the marble for his sculptures, Michelangelo visited the marble quarries in the mountains above Carrara, on the northern coast of Tuscany.

The **Tondo Doni**

This tempera on wood painting commemorating a birth (now at the Uffizi, Florence) was executed by Michelangelo between 1504 and 1506 and has a diameter of 120 cm (4 ft.). It is perhaps the only finished work on wood that the artist produced. In it Michelangelo applies the classical principle known as "contrapposto" (counterpoise) —the balanced arrangement of bodies, arms and legs in a serpentine line—which the artist also used in the David *and the figures of the Sistine chapel.*

Life

Michelangelo Buonarroti was born in Caprese, near Arezzo, in 1475. In 1488 he was an apprentice in the workshop of Ghirlandaio. Later, attracted by sculpture, he joined the circle of Lorenzo de' Medici. In 1492 he sculpted the *Battle of the Centaurs* and in 1496, in Rome for the first time, he sculpted the *Bacchus*. In 1504 he executed the *David* for the Florentine Republic, and in 1505 Julius II summoned him to Rome to execute Julius' funerary monument. From 1508 to 1512 he frescoed the ceiling of the Sistine chapel. From 1516, he worked in the Florentine church of San Lorenzo for Pope Leo X de' Medici. In 1534 he again left Florence for Rome. In 1536, Pope Paul III commissioned him to execute the Last Judgement in the Sistine chapel. In 1547 he was supervisor of works in the new basilica of St. Peter's. He died in Rome on February 15, 1564. Above, Raphael, *School of Athens*, 1509–10; fresco, base 770 cm (27 ft.), Vatican Museums, Rome, detail of the portrait of Michelangelo.

Sledging

Marble blocks were transported to the bottom of the valley by a delicate process called "sledging," illustrated here.

The Captives

The four marble statues that Michelangelo originally intended for the tomb of Julius II della Rovere have been called "slaves" or "captives" because they seem to be imprisoned in the material from which they are carved. Left, Bearded Captive, *1513–20; height 263 cm (8 ft., 8 in.), Galleria dell'Accademia, Florence.*

Raphael, *Portrait of Julius II*, 1512; tempera on wood, 108.5 x 80 cm (42.75 x 31.5 in.), Uffizi, Florence, detail.

Rome in the early 16th century

The Spanish had taken the Kingdom of Naples, the French the Duchy of Milan; in the middle were the Papal States with the pope as the arbitrator of Italian politics. Julius II fought against Venice and the French. His successors were two members of the Medici family: Leo X (1513–1521) and — after the brief papacy of Adrian VI — Clement VII (1523–34), who supported France. In retaliation, Charles V ordered the sack of Rome in 1527.

Titian, *Pope Paul III with Alessandro and Ottavio Farnese*, 1546; oil on canvas, 210 x 174 cm (6 ft., 10 in. x 5 ft., 8 in.), Capodimonte Gallery, Naples, detail.

The tomb

Michelangelo, Tomb of Julius II, 1512–45; marble, San Pietro in Vincoli, Rome. The tomb was finally built after 33 years of endless dispute.

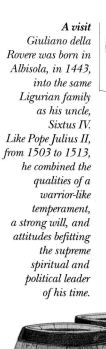

Moses

Generally dated 1515, the marble statue is 235 cm (7 ft., 8.5 in.) high. The figure of Moses, seated in the central niche, is at the center of the whole composition. According to some scholars, it is the only part of the Tomb of Julius II *that can safely be attributed to Michelangelo.*

Bramante

Donato Bramante's "tempietto" (San Pietro in Montorio, Rome), one of the symbols of the Renaissance, was built in c. 1502–10 on the site of St. Peter's martyrdom.

A visit

Giuliano della Rovere was born in Albisola, in 1443, into the same Ligurian family as his uncle, Sixtus IV. Like Pope Julius II, from 1503 to 1513, he combined the qualities of a warrior-like temperament, a strong will, and attitudes befitting the supreme spiritual and political leader of his time.

Julius II

In 1505 Pope Julius II, the nephew of Sixtus IV, called Michelangelo to Rome to design his monumental tomb. This ill-fated project, fraught with numerous difficulties and endlessly postponed, was to become the torment of the artist's life. At the court of the Renaissance pope, Michelangelo met the young Umbrian painter Raphael, but came into conflict with both the architect Bramante and Julius II himself. Before long he had returned to Florence, but the pope succeeded in persuading the Florentine Republic to send him back. In Rome, Julius II invited Michelangelo to take on the great project of frescoing the entire ceiling of the Sistine chapel, replacing the starry sky wanted by Sixtus IV.

The scaffolding
Bramante
had designed a
suspended platform,
but Michelangelo
replaced it with a
platform that was
tiered on two sides
and rested on beams
inserted into existing
openings and
supported by other
beams resting on the
cornice of the walls.

The cartoons

In May 1508, Michelangelo—who considered himself more of a sculptor than a painter—rather reluctantly accepted the commission he had received from Pope Julius II to decorate the lunettes and ceiling of the Sistine chapel. He summoned various assistants from Florence and devoted the first months of work to the preparation of the cartoons. Cartoons are full-scale drawings of the final composition, executed on large sheets of heavy paper. For convenience, the cartoons are cut into sections whose shapes coincide with the areas that are systematically painted to produce the overall work. In August the cartoons were taken to the top of the scaffolding, lying just under half the area of the vault, and work on the ceiling decoration began.

The "arriccio"
An assistant applies a first layer of rough plaster, 1 inch thick, made of lime and pozzolana.

Marking out
Over the "arriccio" two assistants mark out the edges of the areas that will be frescoed by Michelangelo. For this they pluck a length of taut cord dipped in paint.

Pricking the cartoon
Small perforations are pricked into the main lines of the drawing. Protected by a second sheet, the cartoon is then laid against the plaster so that the drawing can be transferred to the wall with the dusting technique known as pouncing.

The cartoons
These are large enough to contain the figures that the artist will fresco. Before working on them, the sheets are cut into sections.

A day's work

The main technique for painting walls and ceilings was *buon fresco*, the laying on of colors to freshly applied plaster. As plaster dries, calcium carbonate is formed, which fixes the pigments, ensuring the colors will not fade. Artists, therefore, could paint only a limited area of plaster at a time, using the few hours available before the plaster dried. This painted portion was called a *giornata* (the Italian word for "day"). Over the first coat of coarse plaster, the *arriccio*, Michelangelo's assistants applied a smoother layer called the *intonachino*. Then the outlines of preparatory drawings were transferred to the plaster, either by pouncing or by cutting. At times, Michelangelo frescoed without the help of cartoons.

The "giornata"
Michelangelo is busy painting a "giornata," the portion of the fresco coinciding with the area of ceiling where fresh plaster has been applied.

Pigments
One of the jobs usually assigned to assistants was the grinding and mixing of pigments.

Pouncing
The small holes that
have been pricked
along the outlines of
the drawing are
dusted with charcoal
powder, which shows
up as a series of dots
on the plaster
surface beneath.
This serves as a
reference for the
painter.

Michelangelo
Creation of Adam,
detail.

Michelangelo's workshop

Fresco painting, a
technique dating
from antiquity, was
taken up in Italy in
the 13th and 14th
centuries. Its
widespread
popularity
coincided with the
establishment of
Florentine
workshops, from
Giotto's onwards.
In the workshops
there was close
collaboration
between the master
and pupils. Painting
was shared among
the pupils, who
were sometimes
asked to paint
secondary figures in
their master's
works. Restoration
of fresco cycles
often reveals the
individual styles of
different painters
who participated in
a project.
This was not the
case with
Michelangelo.
At the beginning,
in 1508, he called
on artists who had
trained in the
Florentine
workshop of
Ghirlandaio—
Francesco
Granacci, Giuliano
Bugiardini,
Aristotele da
Sangallo, Agnolo
di Donnino and
Jacopo di
Sandro—but the
painting he asked
them to do was
minimal.

The "intonachino"
An assistant applies
a final layer of
smooth plaster,
½ inch thick,
made from a
mixture of lime
and pozzolana.

Fresco painting

Michelangelo tackled the painting of the Sistine ceiling in two stages, proceeding initially from the entrance wall towards the altar, that is, in the opposite direction to the narrative sequence of the central stories. The second half of the ceiling, painted between 1511 and 1512, is usually regarded as a more mature expression of his style. This is confirmed by the larger size, and therefore small number, of daily sections (*giornate*) into which the painting is divided. During this stage, the cartoons were transferred to the plaster with the method of indirect incision. Michelangelo's great precision is reflected in his use of measured brush-strokes and a careful choice of colors. He used pigments that were most suited to painting *a fresco*, avoiding those that were vulnerable to deterioration, and it is believed he made very limited use of retouchings *a secco*, traditionally used for corrections and for highlighting details when the plaster was dry.

Lighting
The scaffolding blocked out the natural light coming from the windows. Michelangelo worked by the light of candles and oil-lamps.

Painting "a fresco"
The pigments mix with the lime of the plaster and dry with it within a few hours, depending on seasonal conditions. It has been calculated that a fresco painter has six hours at his disposal, the two hours in the middle yielding the best results. Fresco painting is one of the most difficult techniques because it leaves no room for error or rethinking. In the Sistine chapel some art scholars have mistaken the pigments and glues used by later restorers for the "a secco" retouchings of Michelangelo, which were in fact extremely limited.

Michelangelo,
Creation of Adam,
detail.

Michelangelo alone
For a year Michelangelo and his assistants worked on the first half of the ceiling. Cartoons were transferred to the plaster with the pouncing technique and retouchings *a secco* were made. From 1509 the best assistants returned to Florence and were replaced by less-experienced apprentices. In his contract with Julius II, Michelangelo had been granted the freedom to choose the subject matter for the decoration, and in fact it was he who modified the pope's original idea of portraying the twelve apostles. The artist's preference for freedom of action was also shown in his work. The surfaces of the *giornate* became larger and as a result their number diminished. After overcoming further tensions with the pope, Michelangelo returned to Rome after a spell in Florence and rapidly completed the work.

Nudes
Flanking the five smaller panels in the center of the ceiling are pairs of nude

youths with oak leaves and acorns, symbols of the powerful Della Rovere family.

The central stories
Nine panels in the center of the ceiling, four larger ones and five smaller ones,

separated by architectural bands, are occupied by episodes from the Book of Genesis.

Medallions
In the cornices of the five smaller panels containing the central stories, the drapery behind the

nude youths passes through the rims of ten bronze medallions representing episodes from the Old Testament.

The ceiling

The decoration of the lunettes and ceiling of the Sistine chapel is composed mainly of scenes drawn from the Old Testament. How free was Michelangelo in his choice of the subject matter? Certainly he was a cultivated man, involved in the political and theological debates of his time. But probably he was also influenced by the need to continue the decorative program already started by Sixtus IV and by the advice of contemporary theologians. The surface frescoed by Michelangelo is divided into three areas: the high part of the walls occupied by the lunettes; the outer fasciae of the ceiling occupied by the spandrels, prophets and sibyls, and pendentives; and the central part of the ceiling occupied by the nine panels representing episodes from the Book of Genesis.

Pendentives
In the pendentives in the corners of the ceiling are four biblical episodes representing the miraculous salvation of the chosen people.

Spandrels
The eight triangular spandrels above the lunettes represent the ancestors of Christ, as listed in the Gospel according to St. Matthew.

Sibyls and prophets
Between the spandrels and the pendentives are the figures of five sibyls from classical antiquity who prophesied the coming of a savior, and seven prophets who prophesied the coming of Christ.

Lunettes
Above the third cornice of the walls, fourteen large semicircular surfaces are frescoed with the ancestors of Christ.

The frescoed surface
Adding up the areas frescoed by Michelangelo between 1508 and 1512 gives a total surface area of 1,196 sq. yds. The frescoed area of the high part of the walls, comprising the lunettes, is in fact 299 sq. yds., while the frescoes of the ceiling cover 897 sq. yds.

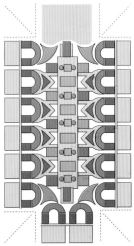

Key

Lunettes

Pendentives

Spandrels

Sibyls

Prophets

Central stories

Medallions

The lunettes

"Abraham begat Isaac; and Isaac begat Jacob; and Jacob begat Judas and his brethren. . . ." So begins the Gospel according to Matthew, with a list of Christ's forefathers. In the Sistine chapel the masters of the 15th century frescoed the gallery of the popes, the successors of Christ. Above this gallery, Michelangelo represented the ancestors, including the principal depositaries of the Messianic promises: Abraham and David and their royal descendants. Originally there were sixteen lunettes: two were destroyed to create space for the Last Judgement; the remaining fourteen represent, in order, the forty generations listed by St. Matthew. The names of the ancestors are written in Roman capitals on plaques in the center of the lunettes.

The lunettes
The lunettes are shown here in the order in which they were painted by Michelangelo, from the ancestors nearest to Christ to those furthest back in time. The sequence starts from the entrance to the chapel and alternates between the left and right sides. The first two lunettes are those directly above the entrance. The large semicircular surfaces, each measuring 3.40 x 6.50 m (11 ft., 2 in. x 21 ft., 4 in.) are broken in the lower part by the arches of the chapel windows.

3. Achim - Eliud

4. Azor - Sadoc

1. Jacob - Joseph

5. Zorobabel - Abiud - Eliakim

2. Eleazar - Matthan

6. Josias - Jechonias - Salathiel

7. Ozias - Joatham - Achaz

11. Salmon - Booz - Obed

8. Ezekias - Manasses - Amon

12. Jesse - David - Solomon

9. Roboam - Abia

13. Aminadab

10. Asa - Josaphat - Joram

14. Naasson

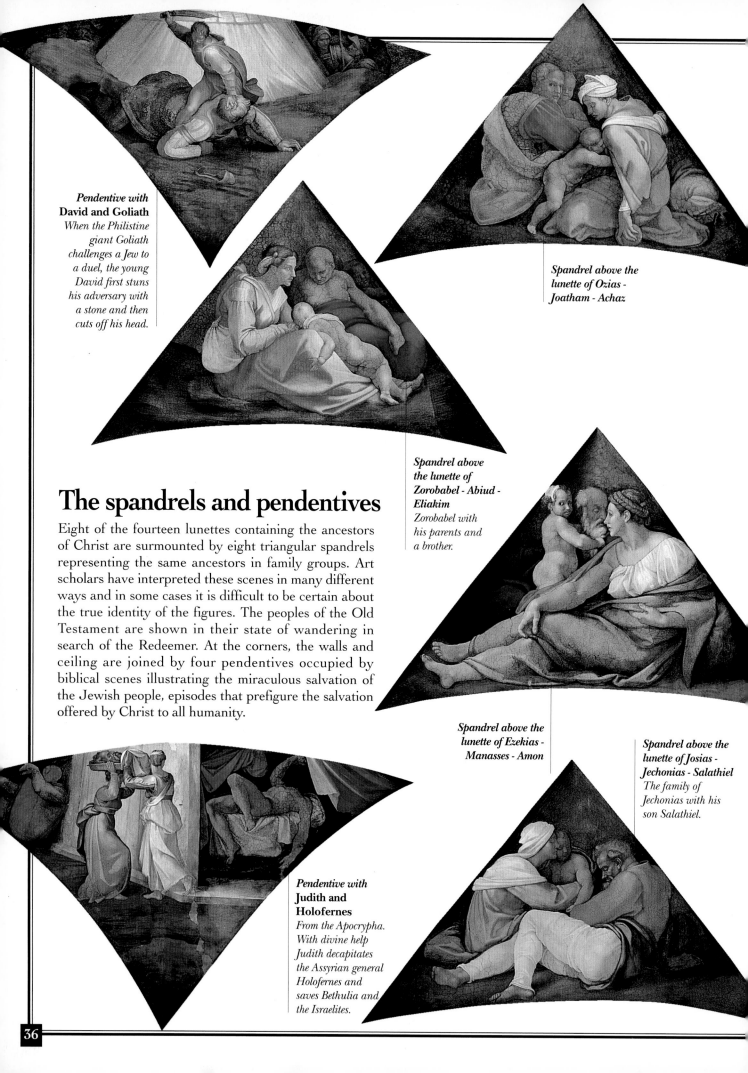

Pendentive with David and Goliath
When the Philistine giant Goliath challenges a Jew to a duel, the young David first stuns his adversary with a stone and then cuts off his head.

Spandrel above the lunette of Ozias - Joatham - Achaz

The spandrels and pendentives

Eight of the fourteen lunettes containing the ancestors of Christ are surmounted by eight triangular spandrels representing the same ancestors in family groups. Art scholars have interpreted these scenes in many different ways and in some cases it is difficult to be certain about the true identity of the figures. The peoples of the Old Testament are shown in their state of wandering in search of the Redeemer. At the corners, the walls and ceiling are joined by four pendentives occupied by biblical scenes illustrating the miraculous salvation of the Jewish people, episodes that prefigure the salvation offered by Christ to all humanity.

Spandrel above the lunette of Zorobabel - Abiud - Eliakim
Zorobabel with his parents and a brother.

Spandrel above the lunette of Ezekias - Manasses - Amon

Spandrel above the lunette of Josias - Jechonias - Salathiel
The family of Jechonias with his son Salathiel.

Pendentive with Judith and Holofernes
From the Apocrypha. With divine help Judith decapitates the Assyrian general Holofernes and saves Bethulia and the Israelites.

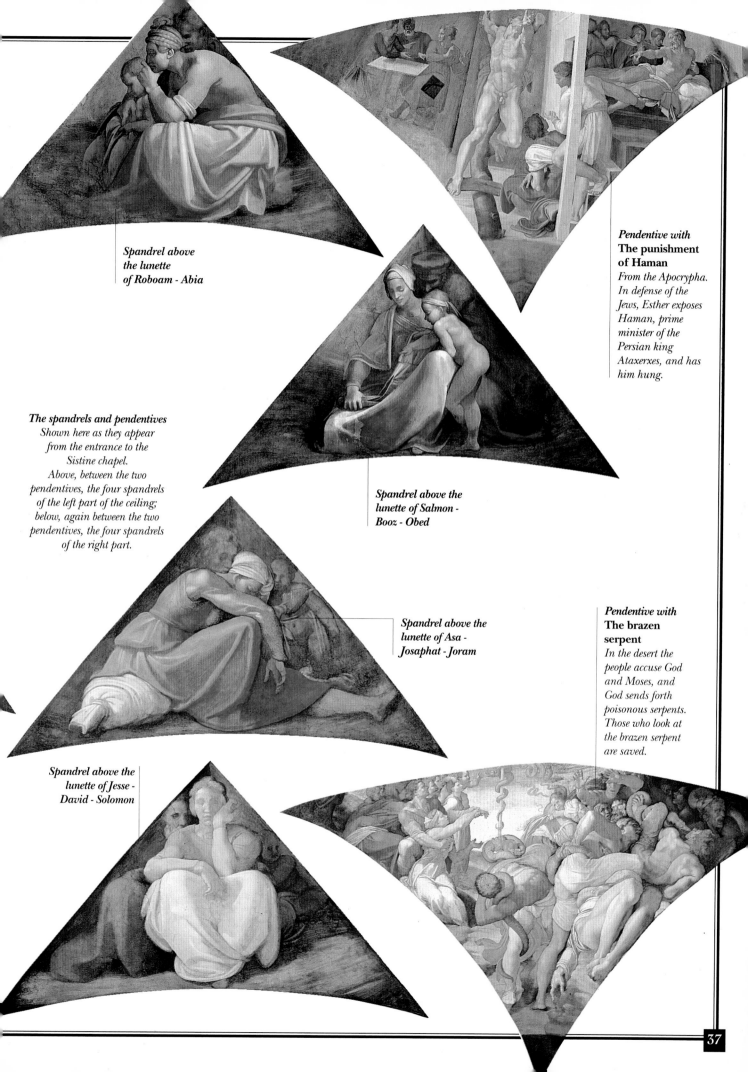

*Spandrel above
the lunette
of Roboam - Abia*

Pendentive with
**The punishment
of Haman**
*From the Apocrypha.
In defense of the
Jews, Esther exposes
Haman, prime
minister of the
Persian king
Ataxerxes, and has
him hung.*

The spandrels and pendentives
Shown here as they appear
from the entrance to the
Sistine chapel.
Above, between the two
pendentives, the four spandrels
of the left part of the ceiling;
below, again between the two
pendentives, the four spandrels
of the right part.

*Spandrel above the
lunette of Salmon -
Booz - Obed*

*Spandrel above the
lunette of Asa -
Josaphat - Joram*

Pendentive with
**The brazen
serpent**
*In the desert the
people accuse God
and Moses, and
God sends forth
poisonous serpents.
Those who look at
the brazen serpent
are saved.*

*Spandrel above the
lunette of Jesse -
David - Solomon*

The sibyls and prophets

Sibyls were the pagan prophetesses of antiquity, and as such were not mentioned in the Old Testament. Their presence in the decoration of the Sistine chapel, together with the prophets of the Jewish tradition, is explained by the tendency that was particularly strong during the Renaissance toward reconciling Christianity with the culture of the classical world. According to Renaissance thought, therefore, Michelangelo was responsible for linking Greco-Roman culture with the world of Judaism and Christianity. The five sibyls alternate with seven prophets. In the Bible the prophets spoke to the people of Israel in God's name and kept alive the expectation of the coming of the Messiah.

1

Delphian Sibyl
The most famous sibyl of the ancient world because of her association with the most venerated pan-Hellenic oracle at Delphi.
Hers is one of the most celebrated figures in the decoration of the Sistine chapel— the beautiful eyes gazing in a direction that balances the opposing rotation of the body.

2

The sibyls
The Erythrean (2), Cumaean (3), Persian (4) and Libyan (5) sibyls were some of the most celebrated prophetesses of antiquity. Michelangelo renders each of the figures with a highly expressive rotatory movement of the body.
The old Persian sibyl, for example, is particularly interesting: the movement of the body, hinging on the elbow, is extremely slow, and the spectator is immediately made aware of the woman's intense concentration as she reads her book. Attention is also drawn to her profile, which reveals nothing of the facial features, but is nonetheless extremely powerful. Lastly, the hunched back seems almost to be generated by the movement of the body. As with numerous other figures, we are again struck by Michelangelo's remarkable ability to represent the human form.

3

4

5

1

Many theories have been advanced to explain the presence and position of each of the seven prophets. The position of Zechariah (1), nearest the entrance, is associated with his identity as "God's memory." After Joel (2), the next four are the major prophets of the Old Testament: Isaiah (3), Ezekiel (4), Daniel (5) and Jeremiah (6). Jonah (7), behind the altar, has a preeminent position because his life prefigured the death and resurrection of Christ.

2

3

4

5

6

7

The central stories

The nine episodes from the Book of Genesis in the rectangular panels in the center of the chapel ceiling are a majestic celebration of the work of God. According to Christian beliefs, God created the universe, created Man in his own image and likeness and placed him in the center of the world. History before the Law of Moses is illustrated by the expulsion of Adam and Eve, and by the punishment and salvation of Noah. These episodes are a prelude to the age preceding the revelation of the Law, represented in the 15th-century frescoes of the Life of Moses, and that of Christ's Redemption. In creating the nine panels, Michelangelo made the vault of the chapel look like an open ceiling, with nine windows opening onto the heavens.

1. Separation of Light from Darkness
The last panel frescoed by Michelangelo, but the first episode of Genesis, therefore the beginning of the narrative series. God appears in the heavens creating spirals of light.

3. Separation of Land and Water
The beginning of the second day of Genesis. God is seen hovering in a boundless space.

Michelangelo has placed this episode after the previous one in contrast to the order of events in the Book of Genesis.

4. Creation of Adam
Perhaps the most famous scene painted by Michelangelo and one of the most celebrated in western art. According to the Catholic faith, man is made in God's image.

7 and 8. The Sacrifice of Noah and The Deluge
Michelangelo reversed the sequence of the two frescoes compared to the chronology of the two biblical episodes.

2. Creation of the Sun, Moon, and Plants

The second scene from the end wall, that of the altar, even though the episode actually refers to the third and fourth day of Creation. God, on the right, surrounded by angels, gives form to the Sun and the Moon; on the left he makes plants grow in the bare earth.

5

5. Creation of Eve

Placed in the center of the ceiling. God appears for the last time.

6. Original Sin and Expulsion from Earthly Paradise

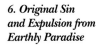

6

9. Drunkenness of Noah

Noah, shown on the left wearing a blood-colored tunic, was the first man to plant a vine. While drunk, he falls asleep naked and is covered with fabric by his sons. Noah's humiliation anticipates the mocking of Christ during the Passion.

9

Looting and destruction

In the early 16th century Julius II's successor, Leo X de' Medici, commissioned Raphael to design the cartoons for ten tapestries that were intended to cover the false curtains forming the lower wall decoration of the chapel. In 1527, during the sack of Rome by the soldiers of the Emperor Charles V, these tapestries temporarily disappeared. Five years earlier, in 1522, the collapse of part of the chapel had destroyed the frescoes of Ghirlandaio and Signorelli representing the two final scenes of the stories of Moses and Christ. These would later be replaced by two works by Matteo da Lecce and Hendrik van den Broek.

The tapestries
Between 1515 and 1517 Raphael made ten cartoons with scenes from the lives of Peter and Paul. These were used by Pieter van Aelst of Brussels to make the tapestries that were hung in the chapel in 1521, stolen in 1527 and finally recovered in 1808. In 1983 (photo above) they were again hung in the Sistine chapel. *Below*, The Miraculous Haul of Fish, *1515; 360 x 400 cm (11 ft., 9.5 in. x 13 ft., 1.5 in.), Vatican Pinacoteca, Rome.*

Raphael, *The Miraculous Haul of Fish*, detail.

The masters
Raphael (Urbino 1483–Rome 1520). Raphael was, with Leonardo and Michelangelo, one of the greatest geniuses of the Renaissance. A pupil of Perugino, he worked in both Florence and Rome, where his masterpiece was the cycle of frescoes for the Vatican "Stanze." He painted many fine portraits and images of the Virgin, including the *Marriage of the Virgin* (Brera, Milan).

Matteo Perez, called Matteo da Lecce (Alezio, Gallipoli ca. 1545–Lima 1615/16). Worked in Rome, where he was a member of the Accademia di San Luca, until 1573; he then moved to Spain and later to Peru, where he became a successful painter and art merchant.

Hendrik van den Broeck (Malines ca. 1519–Rome 1597). Worked first in Antwerp, then for the Medici in Florence, and later in Orvieto and Naples, though his main activity was in Rome under Gregory XIII (1572–85).

The frescoes of the second half of the 16th century
Above, fresco by Matteo da Lecce, Dispute over the Body of Moses; *below, fresco by Hendrik van den* Broeck, Resurrection of Christ. *Completed under Pius V and Gregory XIII, these works replaced Signorelli's* Dispute *and Ghirlandaio's* Resurrection, *which completed the cycle of frescoes representing scenes from the Lives of Moses and Christ. The divine nature of Christ admitted no dispute between Good and Evil, as had happened over the body of Moses.*

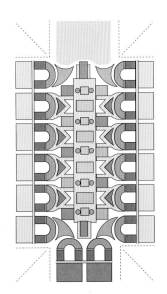

Collapsing wall
During Christmas of 1522, the architrave over the door into the chapel collapsed. Pope Adrian VI had just walked under it. Two guards were killed in the incident and two 15th-century frescoes destroyed.

The work
After the sack of Rome, Pope Clement VII called Michelangelo back to Rome in 1534. His successor, Paul III, confirmed the papal commission to paint a large Last Judgement on the altar wall of the Sistine chapel: it was to measure 13.70 x 12.20 m (45 x 40 ft.). Despite the artist's resistance and the slowness of the preparations, work began in 1536 and continued until the inauguration of the painting on October 31, 1541. Michelangelo was over sixty years old when he started the work. He used the *buon fresco* technique, rejecting any possibility of painting in oils. To make space for the huge fresco, the artist walled up two windows, and destroyed the two frescoes that began the stories of Moses and Christ and an altarpiece by Perugino. Within weeks of its completion, Michelangelo's Last Judgement was attacked by some for being obscene and heretical. But the work that was the cause of such outrage in the 16th century has long been recognized as one of the greatest masterpieces in the history of art.

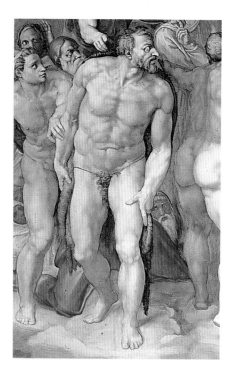

John the Baptist and St. Peter
To the left of Christ, the gigantic figure of St. John the Baptist (left) stands among the blessed. He is balanced, on the other side of Christ, by the equally prominent figure of St. Peter (right). On the day of Judgement Peter—the apostle and direct successor of Christ—gives back the keys, symbol of the popes, which are now unnecessary at the end of time.

The Last Judgement

In 1541, Michelangelo frescoed the entire wall behind the altar with his masterpiece, the Last Judgement. Described in the Gospel of St. Matthew, the subject had already been represented in medieval art, notably by Giotto. However, Michelangelo's version of it is the most famous and that in which the master gives one of the highest expressions of his sculptural conception of the human figure. Christ's imperious gesture and the sound of the angels' trumpets signal the end of time. Christ judges the righteous, who enter the Kingdom of Heaven, while the wicked are condemned and cast into Hell for all eternity. The throngs of figures circling around the figure of the Redeemer in no way disturb the unity of the composition.

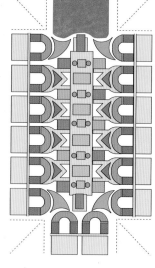

The end of time
The angels' trumpets announce the end of time. The entire history of humankind is represented in the decoration of the Sistine chapel: from the original act of creation, when God separated light from darkness, through the expulsion from paradise, the vicissitudes of the chosen people and the redemption, up until the final act.

The saved
To the sides of the angels, groups of figures rise from the dead, recover their bodies, and are drawn up towards Heaven.

Christ
In the center with the Virgin Mary, surrounded by apostles and saints, by the saved and by figures from the Old Testament.

The angels
In the lower area of the painting, trumpet-blowing angels announce the end of time.

Redemption
In the lunettes at the top of the painting, flying angels carry the instruments of Christ's Passion.

The damned
Driven down into the infernal abyss. Many of the figures make vain attempts to escape their fate.

The 20th century

The Sistine chapel is the pope's chapel, but it is also the place where for over a century new popes have been elected. To avoid the possibility of any interference or pressure from outside, after the death of a pope the members of the college of cardinals who are less than eighty years old withdraw to the Sistine chapel in order to elect his successor. This special meeting is therefore called a conclave, from the Latin *cum clavi*, "behind locked doors." After the election, the new pope receives the vow of obedience from the electing cardinals, again in the Sistine chapel, and then, clothed in traditional white robes, appears on the central balcony of St. Peter's basilica to give his first blessing to the city and to the world.

The stove
The result of the vote is conveyed, by means of a smoke signal, to the congregation assembled in St. Peter's Square. After the ballot the voting-cards are burned in a stove in the Sistine chapel. If a pope has not been elected, black smoke is seen to come out of the chimney; if instead he has been elected, the smoke is white. In the past, the black smoke was made by burning damp straw; now it is made with the help of chemical additives.

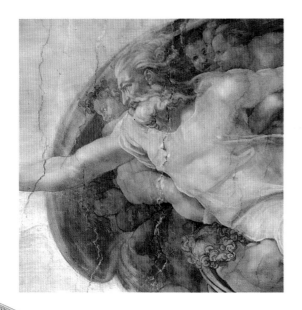

Before and after
The two illustrations show the striking difference between how God appeared before (left) and after the recent cleaning of the ceiling (right).

Restoration
The first cleaning phase was carried out between 1965 and 1974 on the 15th-century frescoes depicting the stories of Moses and Christ. In 1980 it was the turn of the two 16th-century frescoes painted by Van den Broeck and Matteo da Lecce. Between July 1980 and October 1984 Michelangelo's 14 lunettes and the 28 portraits of popes were cleaned. From November 1984 to December 1989 the whole ceiling was cleaned, a project that absorbed 30,000 working hours and involved the use of a special light-weight metal-alloy scaffold. During this time, the restoration was accompanied by international conventions, inspections, photographic studies, and surveys by scholarly commissions. Lastly, from 1990 to 1994, the fresco of the *Last Judgement* was cleaned.

Voting
When a new pope is elected, there are two votes in the morning and two in the afternoon. The rules state that the pope can only be elected with two-thirds of the votes plus one. The ballot is secret.

Index (does not include the names appearing in the titles of works or those of the captions)

Credits

ABBREVIATIONS: a, above; b,
below; c, center; r, right; l, left.
ILLUSTRATIONS:
All the illustrations in the
book and on the front and
back covers were executed for
DoGi spa by L. R. Galante:
©1996, 1997 and 1998 by
DoGi spa, Florence.
REPRODUCTIONS OF THE WORKS:
(The numbers refer to those of
the list of works on p. 3):

Archivio DoGi, Florence: 9,
16, 39, 47, 52, 75; Archivio
DoGi, Florence (Foto
Quattrone): 19, 76; Archivio
DoGi, Florence (Foto Serge
Domingie, Marco Rabatti): 31,
37, 64, 73; Archivio DoGi,
Florence (Foto Saporetti): 4;
Archivio Fotografico dei Musei
Vaticani/T. Okamura: 1;
Archivio Fotografico dei Musei
Vaticani/A. Bracchetti: 15, 70,

74; Archivio Fotografico dei
Musei Vaticani/A. Bracchetti/P.
Zigrossi: 13, 14, 32-36, 38, 40-
46, 48-51, 63, 69, 71; Archivio
Fotografico dei Musei
Vaticani/A. Maranzano: 62;
Archivio Fotografico dei Musei
Vaticani/M. Sarri: 17, 29, 30;
Archivio Fotografico dei Musei
Vaticani/P. Zigrossi: 2, 3, 5-8,
10-12, 18, 20-27, 28, 53-60, 61,
65-68, 72.

**PHOTOS OF INTERIORS AND
EXTERIORS**:
(The numbers refer to the
pages of the book):
Inside: Archivio DoGi,
Florence: 12 a; Archivio
Fotografico dei Musei
Vaticani/A. Bracchetti/P.
Zigrossi: 6bc, 42ar, 47a, b.

The Bryant Library

Roslyn, New York

(516) 621-2240